MUSIC THEORY
LESSONS

For The Very Young Musician

Patricia F. Robinson - The Robinson Method

Dedicated to:
Davel, Daquan, Tyrajah, Micaela, Tyjanae and Malcolm

Thank you to all of you who helped with the book.

Bongo Bob

Piano Pete

Tommy Trumpet

Violet Violin

Dora Drum

Tex Xylophone

Sammy Sax

Hi. I'm Sue the singer
and these are my friends.

Keyboard Chart
Musical Alphabet

Note to Parents and Teachers: This is the musical alphabet. When we get to "G" we start over.

Trace your left hand
Write your finger number names

Note to Parents and Teachers:

The example above is for piano students. If the child is playing another instrument replace the fingering with the appropriate ones.

Trace your right hand

Write your finger number names

1 2 3 4 5

Treble Clef

Notes to Parents and Teachers:

Also called the "G" Clef.

Most small instruments play in the treble clef.

The violin, flute, clarinet and other instruments who play high tones use the treble clef.

The right hand plays the treble clef on the piano.

G clef

This is a Treble Clef.
It is also called
a "G" Clef.

Treble Clef

Bass Clef

Notes to Parents and Teachers:

Also called the "F" Clef.

Instruments that use the bass clef are big and play low tones.

The bassoon, string bass, trombone, tuba, piano and others use the bass clef.

The left hand plays in the bass clef on the piano.

Whole Note

Notes to Parents and Teachers:

The whole note gets 4 counts.

It looks like a circle.

Hold the note for 4 counts.

Whole Note

A whole note looks like a circle. It gets 4 counts.

4

○

◆◆◆◆ counts

Half Note

Notes to Parents and Teachers:

The Half Note gets 2 counts.

It is a circle with a stem.

The stem can be on the left or the right side of the note.

It takes 2 half notes to equal the whole note.

Dotted Half Note

Notes to Parents and Teachers:

The Dotted Half Note gets 3 counts.

It is a circle with a stem and a dot.

The stem can be on the left or the right side of the note.

The dot adds half the value of the note to the note.

The note gets 2 counts and the dot gets 1.

3 counts

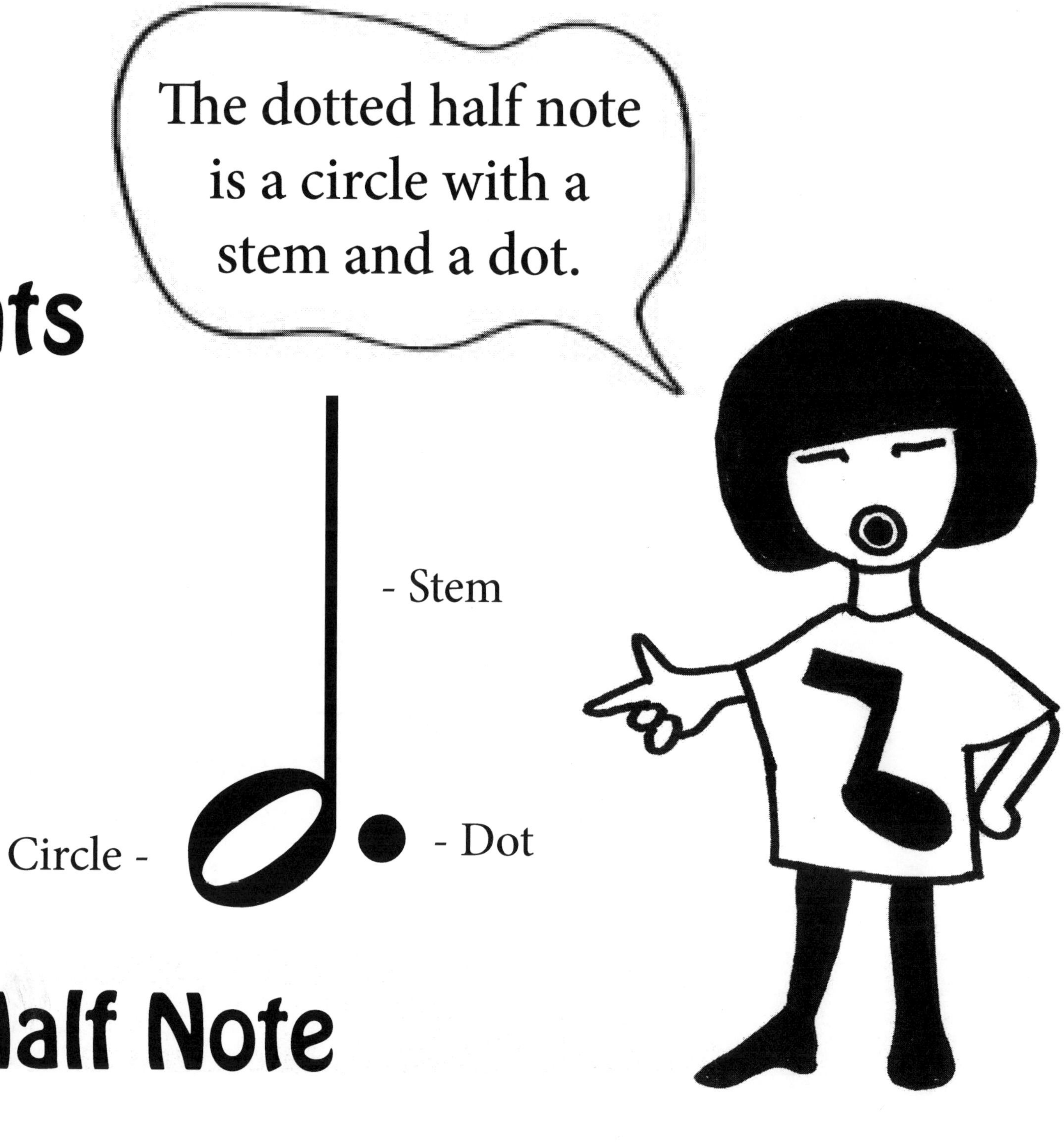

Dotted Half Note

Quarter Note

Notes to Parents and Teachers:

The Quarter Note gets 1 count.

It is a circle that is blackened in with a stem.

The stem can be on the left or the right side of the note.

It takes 4 quarter notes to equal a whole note.

3 quarter notes equal a dotted half note and

2 quarter notes equal a half note.

Quarter Note

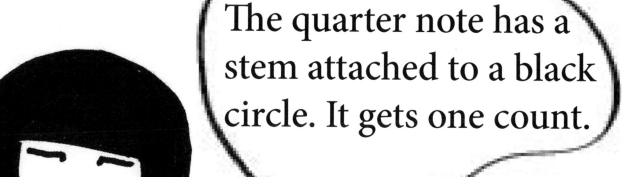

The quarter note has a stem attached to a black circle. It gets one count.

1

◆ count

- Stem

Black Circle -

Theory Lesson 1

Notes to Parents and Teachers:

The staff has 5 lines and 4 spaces.

The notes are drawn on the staff.

Directions:

Trace the 1st line red.

Trace the 2nd line blue.

Trace the 3rd line orange.

Trace the 4th line brown.

Trace the 5th line green.

In music we read from the bottom to the top.

The Staff

5 --

4 --

3 --

2 --

1 --

Notice line 1 is on the bottom.

Theory Lesson 2

Draw whole notes in the first space on the next page.

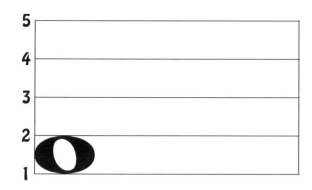

The Staff

The first space is between lines one and two

5

4

3

2

1

Theory Lesson 3

Draw whole notes in the second space on the next page.

The second space is between line 2 and 3

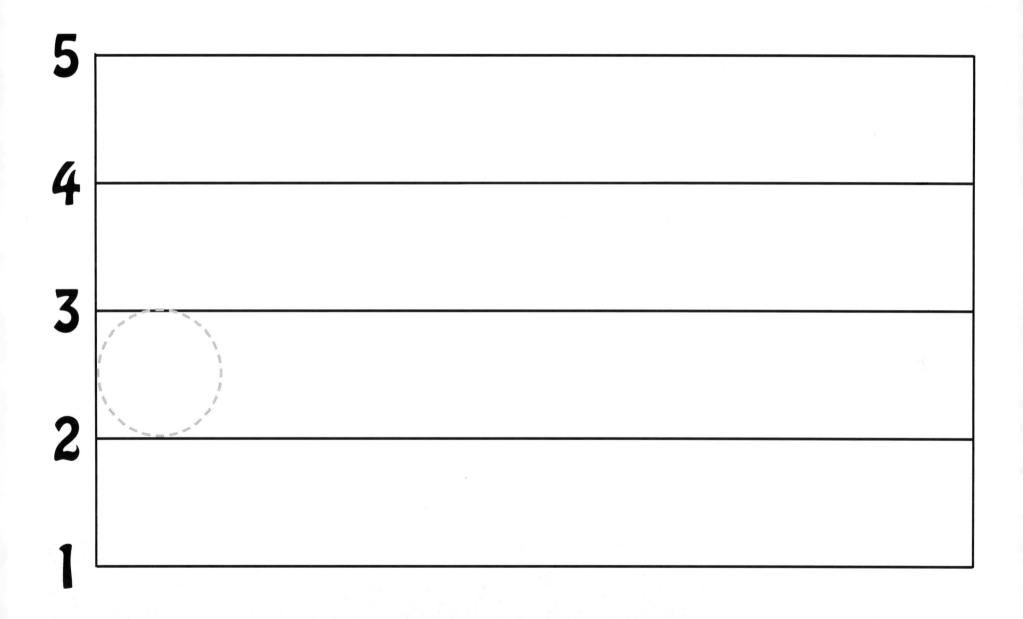

Theory Lesson 4

Draw whole notes in the third space on the next page.

The third space is between lines 3 and 4

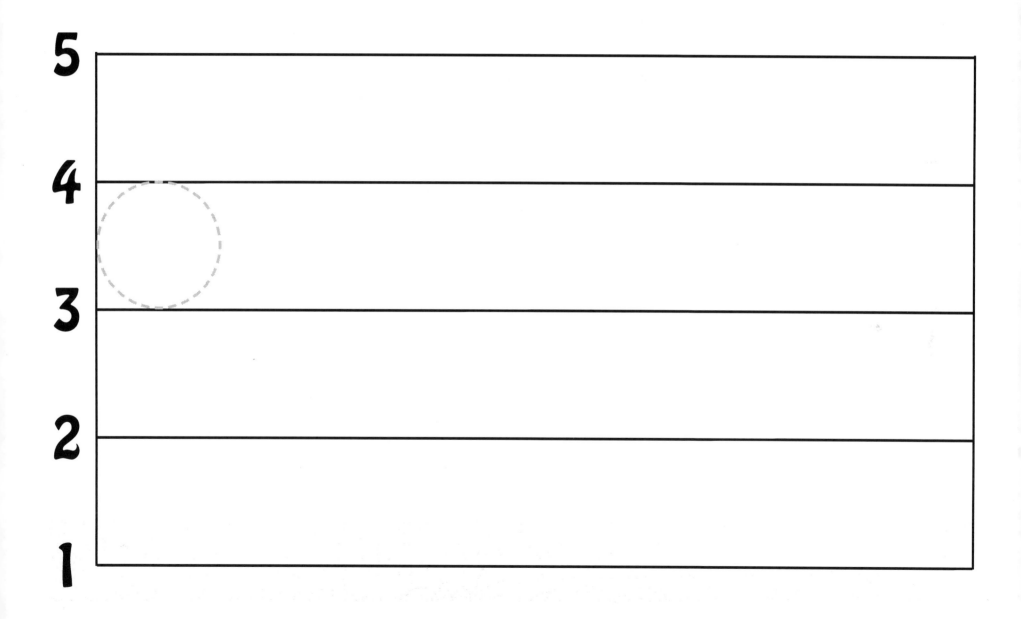

Theory Lesson 5

The fourth space is between lines 4 and 5

Theory Lesson 6

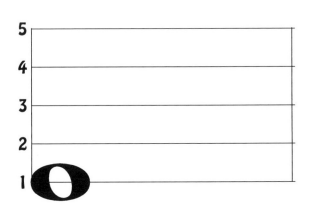

Draw whole notes on the first line on the next page.

TIP: Drawing around specific lines is more complicated than drawing in spaces. Be patient!

Now we're drawing on the first line

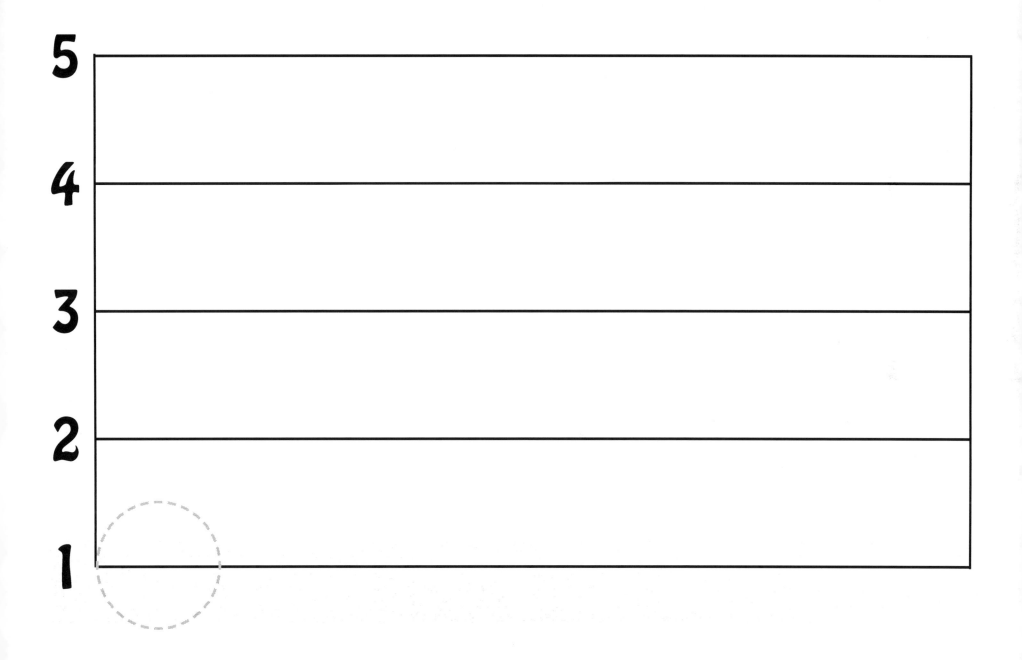

Theory Lesson 7

Draw whole notes on the second line on the next page.

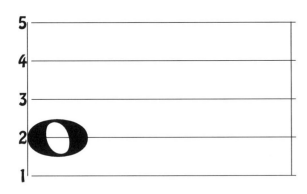

TIP: Don't forget to reward your child with stickers or stars!

Now we're drawing on the second line

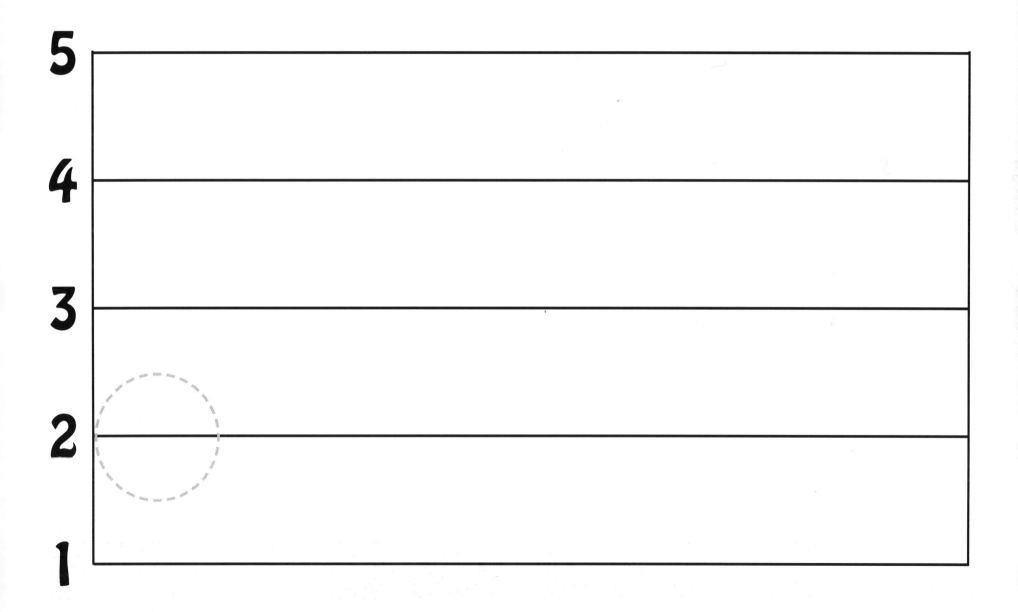

Theory Lesson 8

Draw whole notes on the third line on the next page.

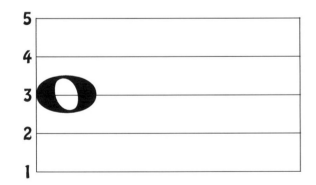

Now we're drawing on the third line

Theory Lesson 9

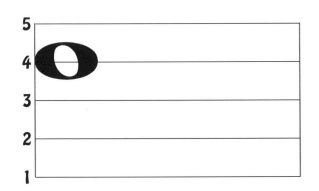

Draw whole notes on the fourth line on the next page.

Now we're drawing on the fourth line

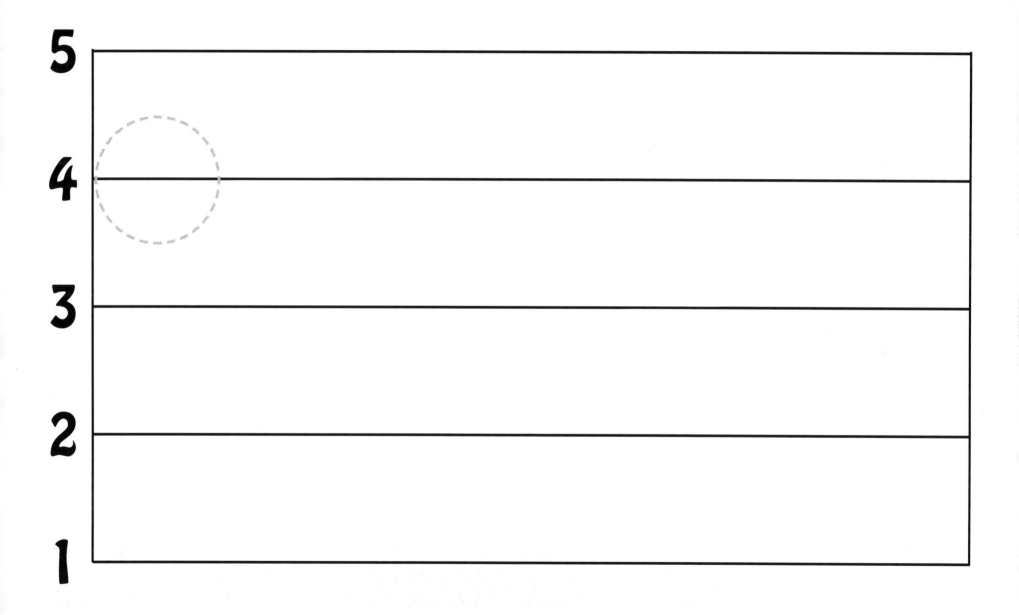

Theory Lesson 10

Draw whole notes on the fifth line on the next page.

Now we're drawing on the fifth line

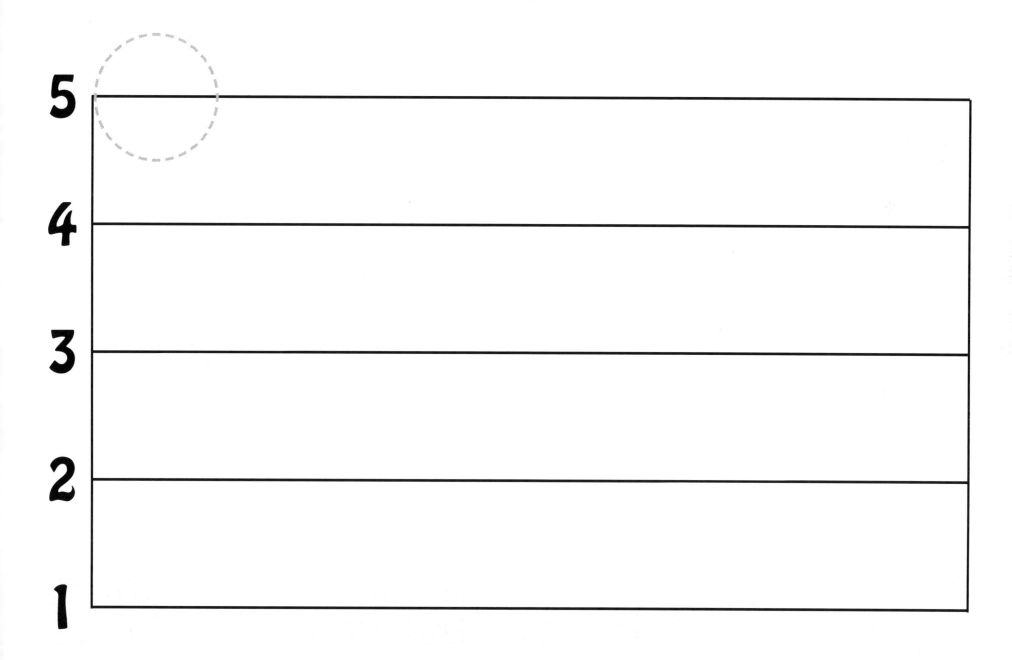

Theory Lesson 11

Draw "C's".
Write the name
under the notes.

C

TIP: Notice the Middle C is not on the staff. It is placed on a leger line below the staff. The student drew circles around the lines on previous pages. The Middle C is a circle within a small line under the staff. Circles and lines are very familiar now.

Now we can play a song!

C three ways

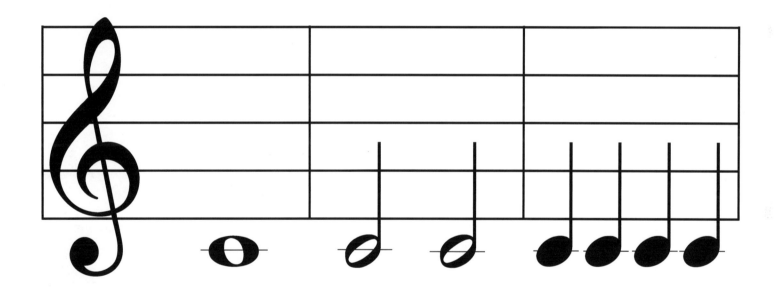

Key finder

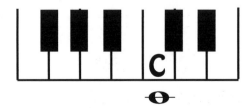

Theory Lesson 12

Draw the note "D". Write the name under the note.

D

NOTE: The note "D" should NOT loop around the line. It MUST touch the line.

D three ways

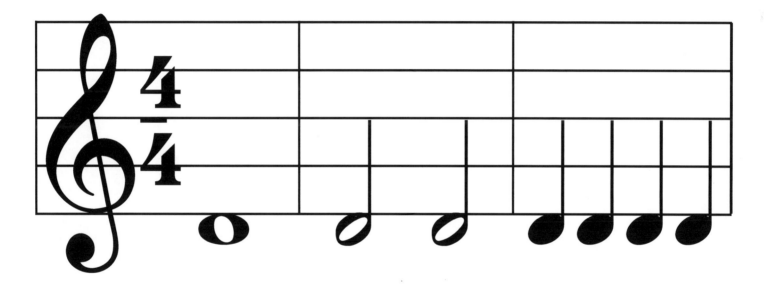

Key finder

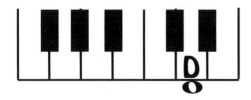

Theory Lesson 13

E

"E" Time

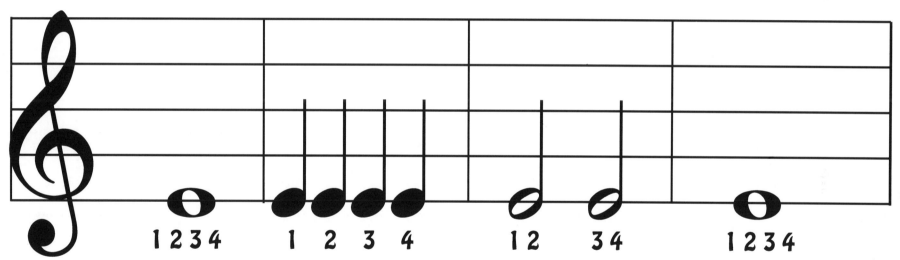

1 2 3 4   1 2 3 4   1 2   3 4   1 2 3 4

Key finder

NOTE: Practice in two ways: 1. Naming the note. 2. Counting the time.

Theory Lesson 14

Draw the note "F"
in the first space.
Write the name
under the note.

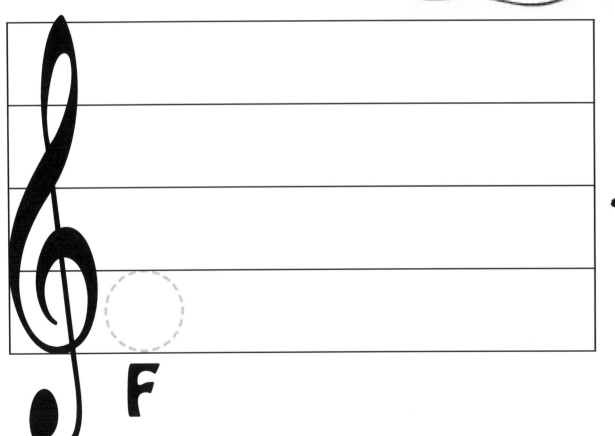

F

Down & Up

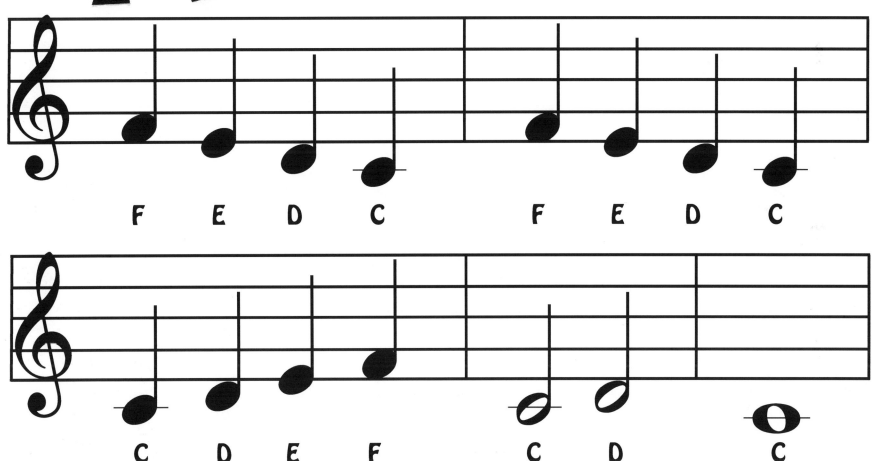

NOTE: Don't forget to name the notes.

Draw the note "G" on the second line. Write the name under the note.

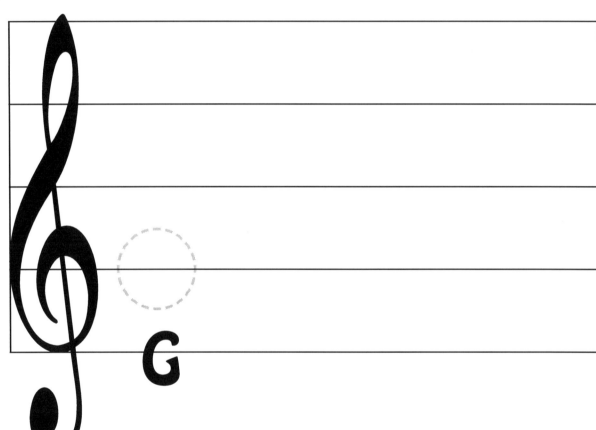

G

Theory Lesson 16

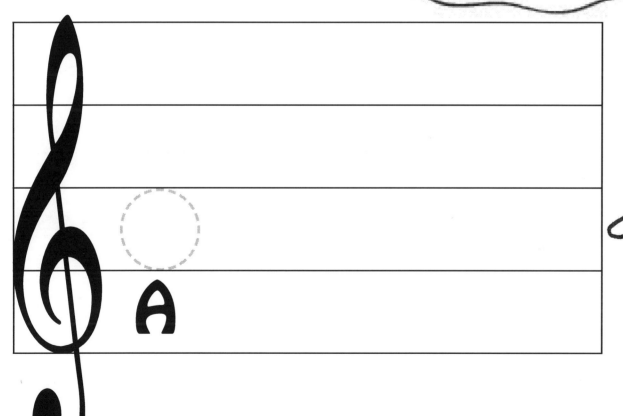

Draw the note "A" in the second space. Write the name under the note.

Theory Lesson 17

Draw the note "B" on the third line. Write the name under the note.

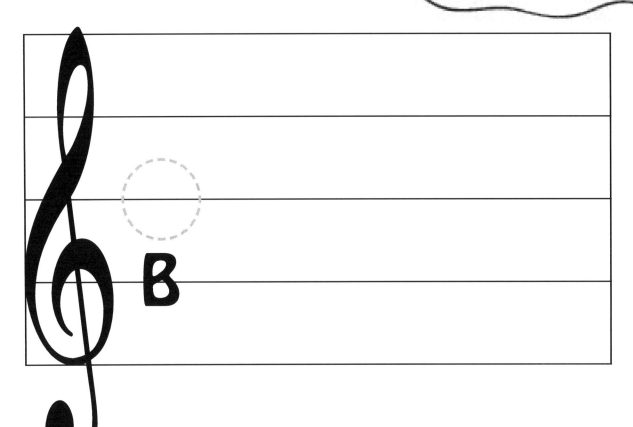

Theory Lesson 18

Draw the note "C" in the third space. Write the name under the note.

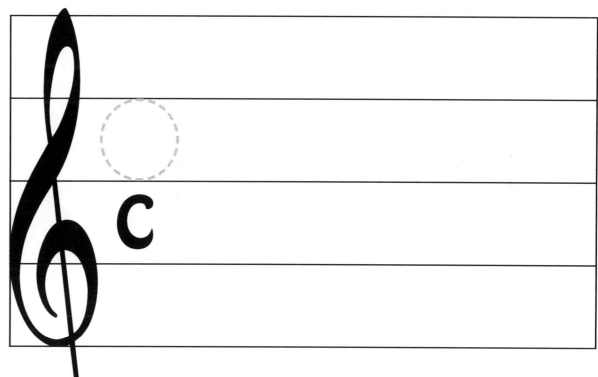

Theory Lesson 19

Draw the note "D" on the fourth line. Write the name under the note.

Theory Lesson 20

Theory Lesson 21

Draw the note "F" on the fifth line. Write the name under the note.

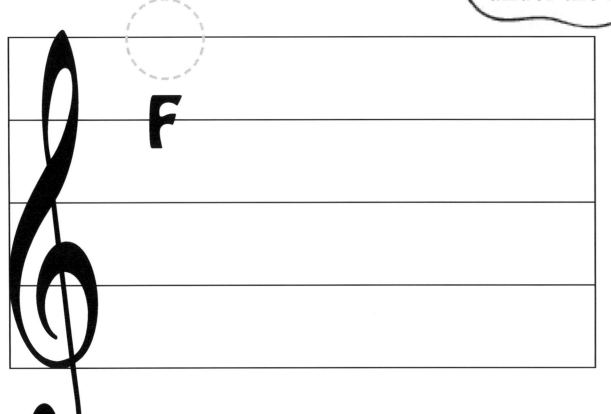

F

Theory Lesson 22

Write the letter name under each note.

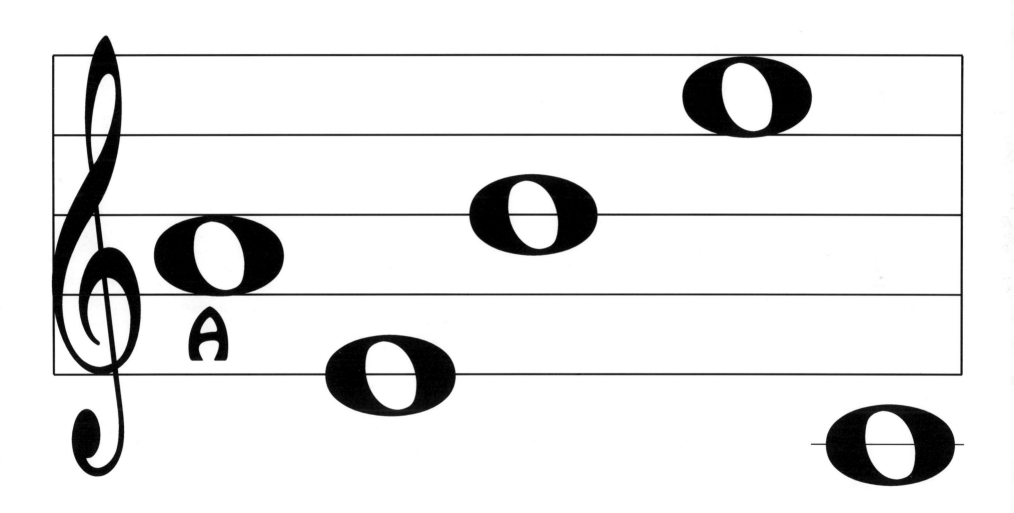

Theory Lesson 23

Write the letter name of each note.

Theory Lesson 24

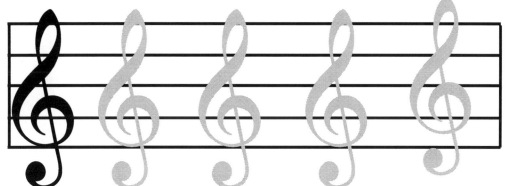

Trace treble clefs on the staves.

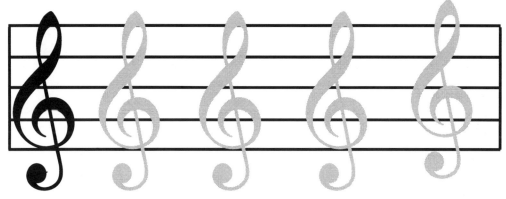

The C Major Scale

Ascending and Descending

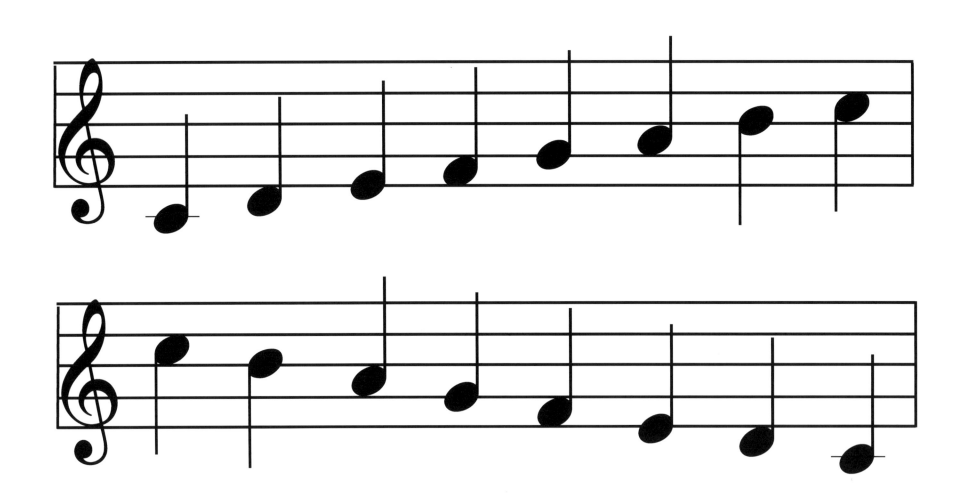

Theory Lesson 25

Trace bass clefs on the staves.

The left hand plays on the bass clef. Middle C is played on the same key as in the right hand.

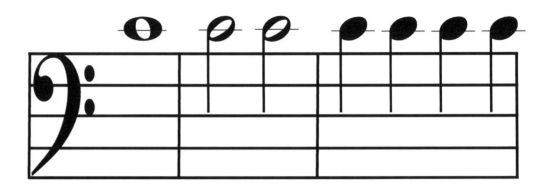

Key finder

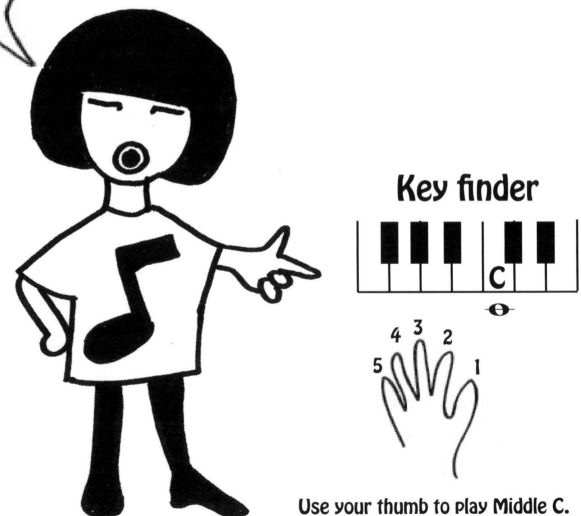

Use your thumb to play Middle C.

Draw the note "Middle C" of the bass clef. Write the name under the note.

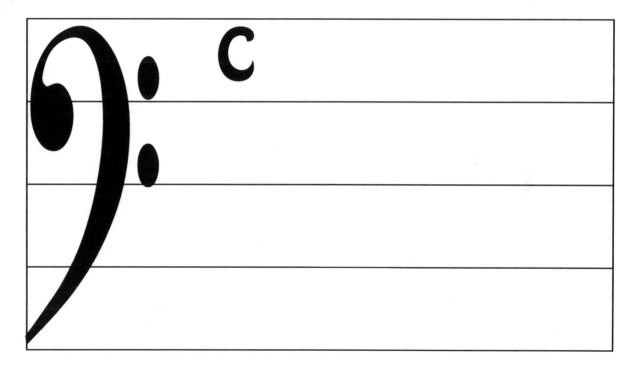

C

Theory Lesson 27

Draw the note "B" of the bass clef on the top of the staff. Write the name under the note.

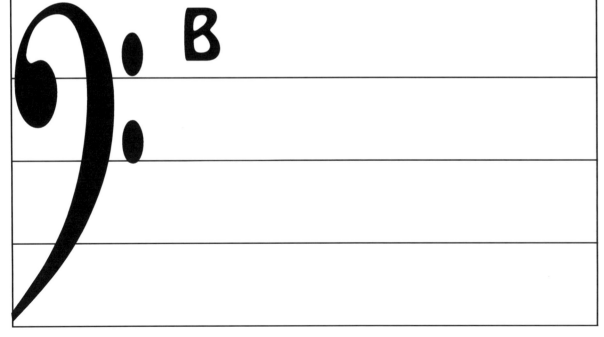

Theory Lesson 28

Draw the note "A" of the bass clef. Write the name under the note.

Theory Lesson 29

Draw the note "G" of the bass clef. Write the name under the note.

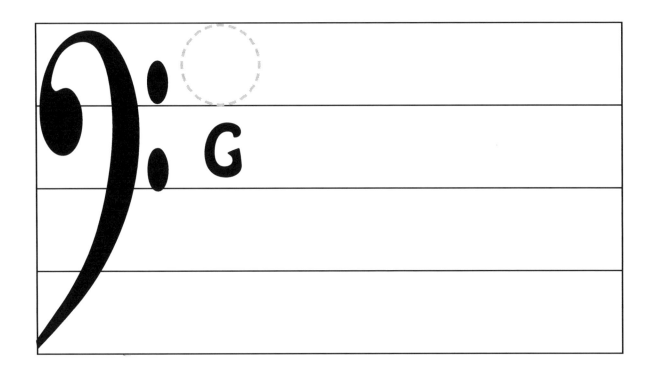

Theory Lesson 30

Draw the note "F" of the bass clef. Write the name under the note.

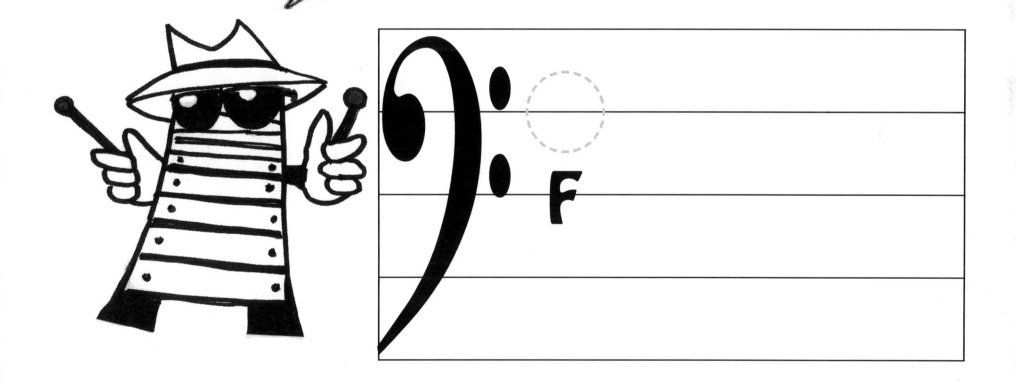

Theory Lesson 31

Draw the note "E" of the bass clef. Write the name under the note.

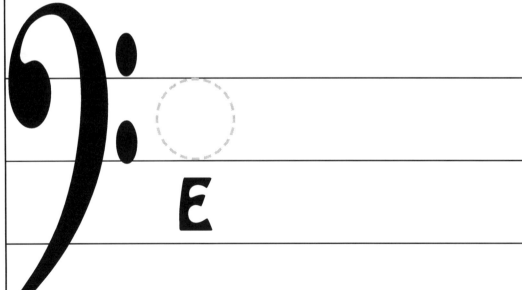

E

Theory Lesson 32

Draw the note "D" of the bass clef. Write the name under the note.

Theory Lesson 33

Draw the note "C" of the bass clef. Write the name under the note.

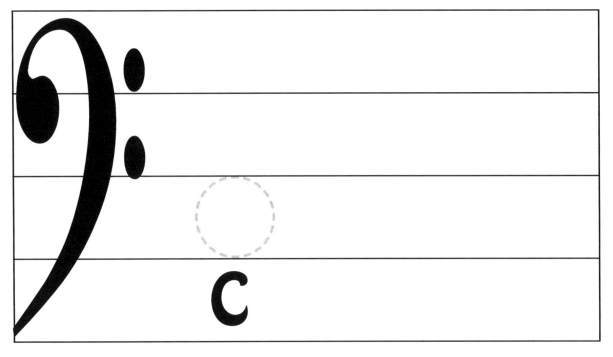

Theory Lesson 34

Draw the note "B" of the bass clef on the second line. Write the name.

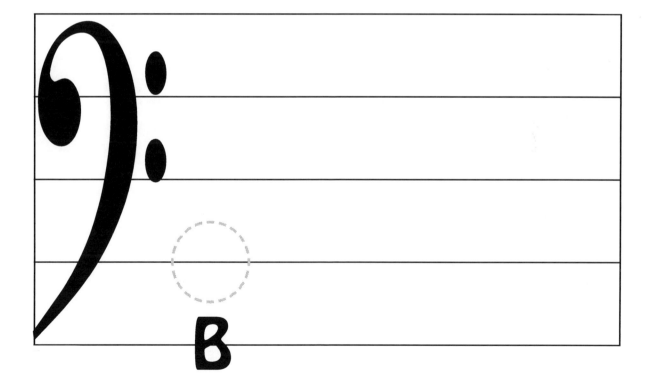

Theory Lesson 35

Draw the note "A" of the bass clef. Write the name.

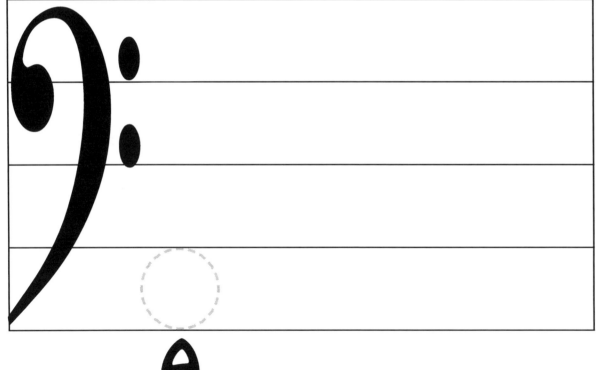

Theory Lesson 36

Draw the note "G" of the bass clef. Write the name.

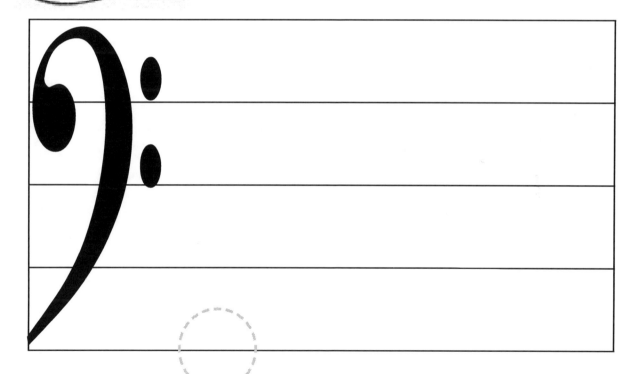

Theory Lesson 37

Write the name under the notes.

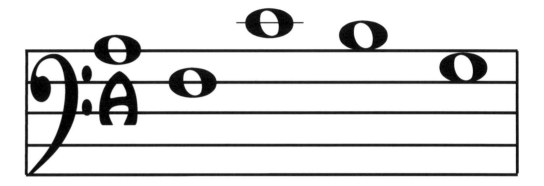

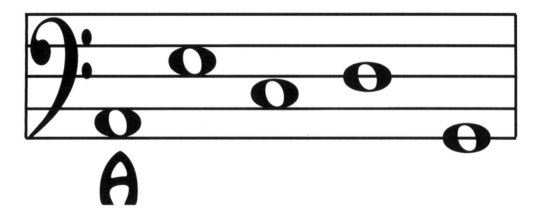

Theory Lesson 38

Write the name under the notes.

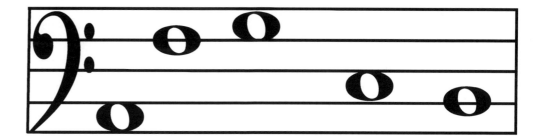

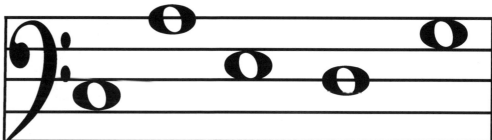

Theory Lesson 39

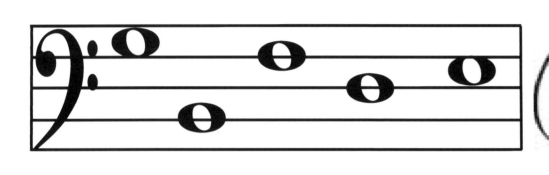

Write the name under the notes.

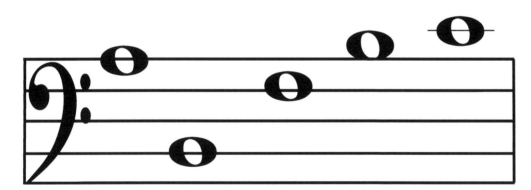

Theory Lesson 40

Draw whole notes on the staff. Write how many counts for each note.

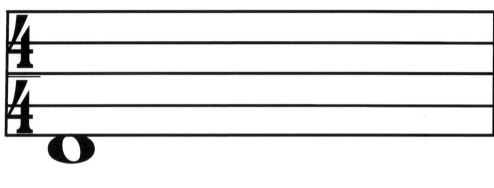

Draw half notes and write the value of each. The half note gets 2 counts.

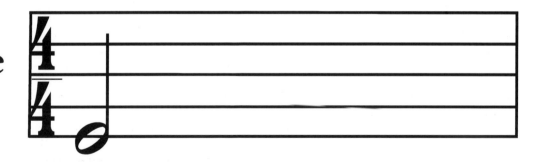

Theory Lesson 41

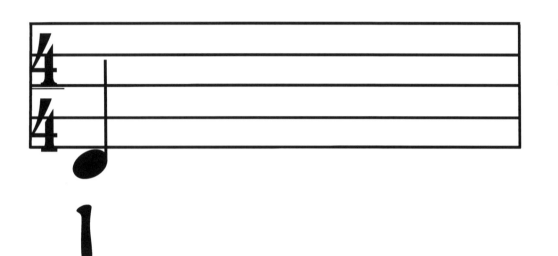

Draw quarter notes on the staff. Write how many counts for each note.

1

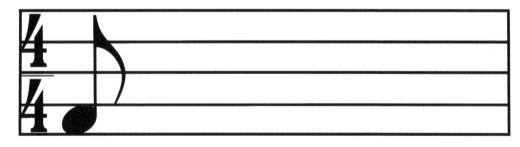

Draw eighth notes and write the value of each. The 8th note gets 1/2 count.

1/2

Theory Lesson 42

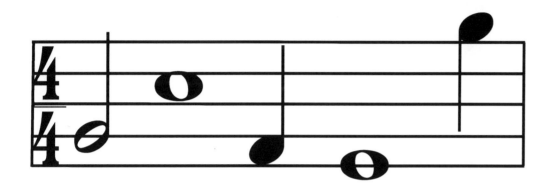

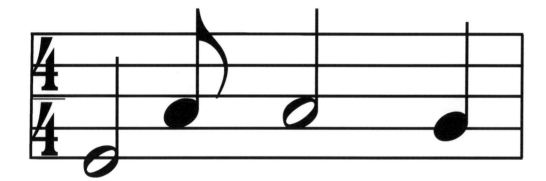

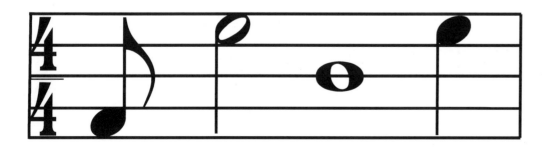

Write the value of each note.

Patricia F. Robinson Music Studio

www.pfrmusicstudio.org

email: pfrmusicschool@gmail.com

Illustrated by: Al Johnson – www.aljohnsonartstudio.com

Design: Mary Z – www.73seegallery.com

13234460R00041